MACMILLAN GUIDED READERS

ELEMENTARY LEVEL

D1807935

WASHINGTON IRVING

The Legends of Sleepy Hollow *and* Rip Van Winkle

Retold by Anne Collins

MACMILLAN

CLASSICS

ELEMENTARY LEVEL

Founding Editor: John Milne

Macmillan Guided Readers provide a choice of enjoyable reading material for all learners of English. The series comprises three categories: MODERN, CLASSIC and ORIGINALS. Macmillan **Classics** are retold versions of internationally recognised literature, published at four levels – Beginner, Elementary, Intermediate and Upper. At **Elementary Level**, the control of content and language has the following main features:

Information Control

Stories have straightforward plots and a restricted number of main characters. Information which is vital to the understanding of the story is clearly presented and repeated when necessary. Difficult allusion and metaphor are avoided and cultural backgrounds are made explicit.

Structure Control

Students will meet those grammatical features which they have already been taught in their elementary course of studies. Other grammatical features occasionally occur with which the students may not be so familiar, but their use is made clear through context and reinforcement. This ensures that the reading as well as being enjoyable provides a continual learning situation for the students. Sentences are kept short – a maximum of two clauses in nearly all cases – and within sentences there is a balance of simple adverbial and adjectival phrases. Great care is taken with pronoun reference.

Vocabulary Control

At **Elementary Level** there is a limited use of a carefully controlled vocabulary of approximately 1,100 basic words. At the same time, students are given some opportunity to meet new or unfamiliar words in contexts where their meaning is obvious. The meaning of words introduced in this way is reinforced by repetition. Help is also given to the students in the form of vivid illustrations which are closely related to the text.

Contents

A Note About the Author

Washington Irving was an American writer. He was born on April 30th, 1783, in New York. As a young man, he studied law and he worked in several law companies. But from 1802, he also wrote stories and essays. At first, these were published in newspapers, but later they were collected together and published in books.

During the years 1804–6, Irving traveled in Europe. He left the United States again in 1815, and he lived in Europe for many years. At first, he worked in a company which was owned by his two brothers, in Liverpool, in England. Eleven years later, he went to live in Madrid, in Spain. He worked for the United States government there. After that, he returned to England for several years, and in 1832, he went back to the United States. His books were now very popular there.

During the years 1842–6, Irving worked in Madrid again. This time, he had a more important government job. Then he returned for the last time to the U.S. He lived in a beautiful house in Tarry Town (Tarrytown), near New York, until his death in 1859.

Irving was the first great American writer of humorous stories. He also wrote books about the countries which he visited, and a book about the life of George Washington—the first U.S. president.

The Legend of Sleepy Hollow and *The Legend of Rip Van Winkle* first appeared in *The Sketch Book*, Irving's most popular book, which was published in 1820.

A Note About These Stories

Dutch people arrived in North America from the Netherlands early in the seventeenth century. They came to live in a new land—they were settlers. Many of them made their homes in the area around the Hudson River, in the east of the land. But at the time when *The Legend of Rip Van Winkle* begins, nearly two hundred years later, this part of North America was a British colony. The land was owned by Britain. The colony was ruled by King George the Third, who was the British king from 1760 to 1820. Some people in North America were happy about this. They liked the British king—they were loyal to King George. But many others did not want their land to be ruled by Britain. They wanted to live in an independent country. They wanted their own government and they wanted their own laws. There was a war between these people and the British army. The Americans won the war, and the British left the colony. At the end of Rip Van Winkle's story, he is living in an independent country—the United States of America. The country has a president, not a king. The first president of the United States was George Washington.

The other story in this book, *The Legend of Sleepy Hollow*, takes place after the war with Britain, early in the nineteenth century.

THE LEGEND OF SLEEPY HOLLOW

1

The Ghost of the Soldier

On the eastern bank of the great Hudson River, in North America, there is a small town. Its name is Tarry Town. Once the town had a different name. Why did it change? This is the reason. Wives often sent their husbands to the market in the town to buy and sell things. "Come back quickly," the wives always said. But the husbands never returned home quickly. They stayed or "tarried" in the town and they drank beer at the inns there. So people started to call the place Tarry Town.

About two miles from Tarry Town is a little hollow—or valley—between some high hills. A small river runs through this valley. The valley is a very peaceful place. Everyone who goes there soon feels peaceful. They quickly forget their troubles. And everyone who lives there always feels sleepy. Because of this strange peaceful feeling, the valley is called "Sleepy Hollow".

Dutch settlers first came to Sleepy Hollow early in the seventeenth century. They made their homes there. But before the Dutch people came, Native Americans had lived there. These people believed in many different spirits. Perhaps these spirits made Sleepy Hollow a strange and mysterious place.

There was something very strange about the people who lived in Sleepy Hollow in the early years of the nineteenth century. They were as peaceful and as sleepy as the valley itself. They believed strongly in God. But they also believed very strongly in ghosts and spirits. They often saw strange things at night. They often heard music in the forest when nobody else was there.

There were many stories about ghosts and spirits in Sleepy Hollow and the area near it. The most famous of these stories was about the ghost of a man on a horse. Lots of people saw the man—that is what they said. He rode a huge black horse, as fast as the wind. He was always seen late at night. And there was something even more terrible about him. He had no head! So the people who lived in the area called him, "The Headless Horseman".

Many people had seen the Headless Horseman late at night. He rode in Sleepy Hollow and he also traveled on the other roads in the area. He was often seen near a small church, a few miles from the valley.

Who was this Headless Horseman? Nobody really knew. But some people told a story about him.

"The Headless Horseman is the ghost of a soldier," they said. "This soldier was killed in the war between Britain and the American colony. There was a terrible battle in this area. In this battle, the soldier's head was shot off by a cannonball from a British gun.

"His body was taken to a little church near the battle-field," these people continued. "It was buried in the graveyard next to the church. But his head still lies somewhere on the battlefield. Every night, the Horseman rides back to the battlefield to look for his head. But he never finds it. And he always has to return to the graveyard before dawn. All ghosts have to go back to their graves before the daylight comes. And the Headless Horseman is always in a hurry because he's always late. That's why he rides so fast."

2

The Schoolmaster

The schoolmaster of Sleepy Hollow was a man named Ichabod Crane. His name was a good one because he looked like the kind of bird which is called a crane. He was very tall and thin, with narrow shoulders and long arms and legs. His head was small, and very flat on the top. He had huge ears, large green eyes and a very long nose. He was not handsome at all.

Ichabod's clothes did not fit him well. They were loose, and they flapped in the wind. So when he walked, the schoolmaster looked very strange.

The school was a low building with one large room, and Ichabod was the only teacher there. This schoolhouse stood by itself at the bottom of the valley. The hills around it were covered with trees. A small river ran near the schoolhouse.

On summer days, the windows of the schoolhouse were always open. Anyone who passed could hear Ichabod's pupils saying their lessons in sleepy voices.

When lessons had finished for the day, Ichabod often went home with one of the children. Some boys and girls had pretty older sisters. Ichabod liked young, pretty ladies. And some of his pupils had mothers who were good cooks. Ichabod liked to go home with these children most of all.

Ichabod was very thin, but he ate a huge amount of food. He loved talking about food and he loved thinking about food. Most of all, he loved eating it.

Ichabod loved food, but he loved singing too. He taught a group of young people to sing psalms—religious songs. Once a week, the group met for psalm-singing lessons. And every Sunday, Ichabod stood with his pupils in the church in the valley and sang psalms with them.

Ichabod had a good life. He did not earn very much money from teaching. He could not buy a house of his own. So he stayed at the houses of different farmers in the area. He stayed with each farmer for a week. Each week, a farmer gave the schoolmaster a bed to sleep in and food to eat. And Ichabod helped the farmers with the work on their farms. He mended fences. He took water to the horses. He cut wood for the farmers' fires. Sometimes he helped the farmers' wives to look after their children.

The farmers' wives were always happy to see Ichabod. They often invited him to tea. They made delicious cakes for him. The young women of the area liked Ichabod too. Sometimes he took walks with them, or read them funny stories. They smiled at him whenever they met him.

All the people of Sleepy Hollow respected Ichabod Crane because he was a schoolmaster. He was clever—he worked with his mind, not with his hands. "He's a very intelligent man," everyone said. Most of the people in the valley could not read or write. But Ichabod *could* read. So he was an important man in the area.

Ichabod Crane believed in God, but he also believed very strongly in ghosts and spirits. On summer evenings, after lessons had finished, he often lay on the grass beside the small river. He lay on the warm grass and read his favorite book. It was a book about ghosts.

Ichabod loved the stories in this book, but they frightened him. He believed everything that he read in them! He often read the book until the sky was dark. Then he could no longer see the pages, so he stopped reading. But then he had to walk back in the dark, to the farmhouse where he was staying.

A forest covered a large part of the area. Often, Ichabod had to walk through the forest to get to the farmhouse. These walks in the dark were terrible for him. He saw ghosts and spirits all around him. The branches of the trees looked like ghostly hands. And they were all trying to grab him.

And there were strange noises in the forest at night. They were really the noises of animals and birds in the trees. But to Ichabod, they were the sounds of evil spirits. Sometimes, his heart beat fast with fear and his legs would not move.

"This is terrible!" he thought, whenever this happened. "There are evil spirits here. They're hiding in the trees and they want to take me away with them. What can I do? I'll sing a psalm. Then the spirits won't be able to hurt me."

So Ichabod often sang a psalm as he walked through the dark forest:

I'm not afraid of ghosts
or evil spirits of the night.
God will always lead me
from the darkness to the light.

The people of Sleepy Hollow often sat outside the doors of their houses in the evenings. They heard the sound of Ichabod's strange, high voice as he passed their homes.

"What's that strange noise?" they asked each other. "Is it a spirit? Oh, no, it's only Ichabod Crane. He's singing as he walks home through the forest!"

On winter evenings, Ichabod sometimes sat with the old women of Sleepy Hollow. He sat by their kitchen fires with them, eating apples and listening to their wonderful ghost stories.

Ichabod's favorite ghost stories were about the Headless Horseman. But when he had to walk home through the forest in the dark winter night, he tried to forget about the stories. He was even more frightened

11

than in the summer.

"Does the terrible Horseman only travel on the roads?" he asked himself. "Or does he haunt the forest too?"

On those dark nights, Ichabod saw the Horseman in every shadow. He heard the noise of the huge black horse in every sound!

3

Ichabod and Katrina

One day, a new pupil joined Ichabod's group of psalm-singers. Her name was Katrina Van Tassel, and she was the daughter of Baltus Van Tassel, an old farmer. Baltus Van Tassel's farm was a few miles from Sleepy Hollow.

Katrina was eighteen years old and she was very beautiful. She had golden blond hair and she liked wearing pretty clothes. All the young men in the area admired Katrina. And Katrina knew this. She enjoyed this admiration very much.

"Katrina is a very pretty girl," said the people of the area. "Her skirts are too short now! But one day, she will be a good wife for somebody. Her husband will be a very lucky man. He will marry Katrina and he'll get her father's farm too."

Katrina was Baltus Van Tassel's only child. She had no brothers or sisters. So when her parents died, Katrina was going to inherit the farm. The land and everything on it was going to be hers. One day, she was going to be rich.

Ichabod Crane liked women. But when he first met

Katrina, he forgot about all other women.

Soon after he met Katrina, Ichabod visited the Van Tassels' farmhouse. It stood in a wide, grassy place on the bank of the Hudson River. As Ichabod rode up to the farmhouse, he saw cows, geese, ducks, turkeys and hens. They all looked very fat and healthy.

At once, Ichabod began to feel hungry. He thought about huge and wonderful dinners.

"Those chickens will taste delicious when they are cooked," he thought. "And those geese and turkeys will be wonderful in pies. And the ducks will be very good with onions."

Then Ichabod looked at all the land which belonged to the farm. He saw fields of golden corn. He saw hundreds of fruit trees, their branches covered with ripe fruit. And when Ichabod saw all these things, he started dreaming about his future life.

"This place is perfect," he said to himself. "If I marry Katrina, I'll have an easy life. I won't have to work. There'll be lots of delicious food all the time. Katrina will take good care of me. I'll be very comfortable here with her and our children.

"Perhaps we'll sell the farm one day," he thought. "We'll get a lot of money and then we'll travel to another part of America."

Ichabod was happy. And when he entered the farm-house, he felt even happier. The kitchen was large, warm and comfortable. There was a wonderful smell of food. There were large baskets full of fruit and vegetables, ready for cooking.

In the living room, the fine wooden furniture shone in the sunlight. The cupboards were full of silver plates and china dishes.

From that time, Ichabod thought day and night about Katrina. "I must marry her," he said to himself. "There's a wonderful life waiting for me on that farm."

4

Brom Bones

But there was a problem for Ichabod. All the young men from the area admired Katrina. And there was one young man who admired her very much. *He* wanted to marry her too. This man's name was Brom Bones.

Brom Bones was very different from Ichabod. He was tall and handsome. His body was big and strong, and he had short, black, curly hair. He was a very brave young man and he was an excellent horse rider. He often rode in horse-races and he always won them.

Brom Bones was not afraid of anybody or anything. He was the leader of a group of young men. These young men admired Brom and they rode with him everywhere. Sometimes the people of the area heard the sound of horses on the road late at night.

"That's Brom Bones and his friends!" they said to each other.

Brom Bones enjoyed playing tricks on people. He was not a bad man, but he liked to have fun.

Brom Bones often went to Baltus Van Tassel's farm to see Katrina. When other young men from the area saw Brom's horse outside the Van Tassels' farmhouse, they smiled sadly.

"Now Katrina won't speak to us," they said. "Brom will win her love easily. And we don't want to fight with Brom."

So everybody else stopped trying to win Katrina's love—everybody except Ichabod Crane.

Ichabod was not worried about Brom Bones and his visits to Katrina. He started to visit her himself. And when the schoolmaster came to the house, Katrina's father smoked his pipe happily. Her mother sang while she did her work. They both smiled when Ichabod took walks with Katrina, or when he sat and talked with her outside the house. All the Van Tassels were happy.

But when Brom Bones heard about Ichabod's visits to Katrina, he was not happy.

"What!" he shouted. "Is that ugly schoolmaster visiting Katrina? I'll fight him. I'll knock him down and put him on a shelf in his own schoolhouse!"

But Ichabod did not want to fight Brom. Brom was very strong and he could win any fight easily—Ichabod knew that. So the schoolmaster stayed away from Brom. This made Brom even more angry.

"I can't fight him with my hands because he won't come near me," Brom said. "So I'll try another way of fighting him."

He started playing tricks on the schoolmaster. First, Brom and his friends got into Ichabod's schoolhouse one night. They moved all the furniture around. Ichabod was very frightened the next day.

"An evil spirit did this," he said.

Next, Brom taught his dog to make a terrible noise. Then he waited outside the schoolhouse with the animal. Whenever Ichabod sang, the dog made this terrible noise. All Ichabod's pupils laughed.

One fine autumn afternoon, Ichabod was in the school-house with his pupils. Suddenly there was a knock at the door. When Ichabod opened it, he saw one of Baltus Van Tassel's servants outside.

"You are invited to a party tonight at the Van Tassel farm," said the servant. "Will you come?"

"Oh, yes!" said Ichabod. He was very happy and excited. He also felt very important. Katrina's parents had asked him to a party. So they really did like him. They wanted him to marry their daughter. That was good. And he was going to see Katrina at the party.

He sent his pupils home an hour early that day. They were very surprised by this. It had never happened before!

5

The Party

Ichabod spent a long time getting ready for the party. He had an old black suit of clothes. It was his only suit. He brushed it carefully. When Ichabod looked at himself in a mirror, he was very pleased.

"How handsome I look," he thought. "Tonight, I'll win Katrina's love—I'm sure of that. But I must have a fine horse to ride to the party. Where can I get one? Perhaps I can borrow a horse from Hans Van Ripper."

Hans Van Ripper owned the farm where Ichabod was staying that week. Ichabod asked to borrow a horse from him. The farmer decided to play a trick on the school-master.

"Yes, you can borrow one of my horses, Ichabod," he said. "I'll lend you my best one."

But when Ichabod saw the horse, he was very surprised. It was old and thin, and it had only one eye.

"Is *this* your best horse?" he asked the farmer.

"Yes," replied Hans Van Ripper. "He's very strong and he runs as fast as a bullet from a gun. His name is Gunpowder."

Gunpowder *did* run fast. But he also had a very bad temper. Hans Van Ripper did not tell Ichabod about this. He pointed to the saddle on the horse's back.

"This is my best saddle," the farmer said. "Please take care of it."

Ichabod climbed onto the expensive saddle, and he and Gunpowder started their journey to the Van Tassels' party. Ichabod and the horse were both very thin and they looked very strange together! Ichabod was not a good horse rider. He sat uncomfortably on Gunpowder's back. As he rode, he moved his long thin arms up and down, like a bird's wings. His loose black coat flapped in the wind. He looked like a huge black bird.

It was a beautiful autumn afternoon. The leaves on the trees were red and gold. As Ichabod rode along, he heard the sounds of birds singing. He rode through fields of golden corn, and fields of apple trees. He began to feel hungry. He began to think about cakes and pies.

At last, Ichabod arrived at the Van Tassels' farmhouse. The party had already started and many of the farmers from the area were there with their families. Everybody was dressed in their best clothes. Their clothes were very colorful and bright.

The most beautiful girl at the party was Katrina.

Everybody admired her. She was laughing and talking to the guests. Ichabod looked at her and he smiled.

But soon, the schoolmaster had an unpleasant surprise. Brom Bones was also at the party. He had come on his big black horse, Daredevil. Brom was standing in the middle of a group of his friends. He was telling stories in a loud voice. Everybody was laughing at his stories.

"Oh, no!" thought Ichabod. "Why is *that* man here?"

When Brom Bones saw Ichabod, his face became angry. Ichabod hurried away, into the dining room. And when he entered that room, he forgot about Brom Bones at once. He even forgot about Katrina!

In the dining room, a great table was covered with all kinds of wonderful food. There were dishes of cooked meat. There were plates of cakes and pies. Ichabod started eating at once. As he ate, he looked around the room and smiled.

"One day, all this will be mine," he thought.

At that moment, Katrina's father came towards him.

"Are you enjoying the party, Ichabod?" Van Tassel asked. "Please eat as much as you want. We have plenty of everything."

After the meal, nearly everybody danced. Ichabod liked dancing very much. When he danced, he moved his arms and legs very quickly. He looked very strange! But he did not know this.

"I'm a very good dancer," he told himself.

Ichabod started dancing with Katrina. Soon, everybody in the room was staring at them. Some people began to laugh.

"How strange Ichabod looks," they said to each other. "Why does he dance in that way?"

Brom Bones did not dance. He sat by himself in a corner. He stared angrily at Katrina.

"Brom is jealous because Katrina is dancing with *me*," thought Ichabod. "That's good."

After the dancing had finished, Ichabod felt tired. He joined a group of people by the fire. They were telling stories to each other. Brom Bones was one of the group.

At first, the stories were about the war between Britain and its American colony. But then people started to tell ghost stories. Ichabod listened carefully. He was always very interested in ghost stories.

Several people from Sleepy Hollow were at the party. They started talking about the Headless Horseman.

"The Horseman is riding again," said one man. "Nobody had seen him for a long time. But this month, several people have seen him. Every night now, he rides from the graveyard and he doesn't come back until just before dawn."

"Yes, that's right," said another man. "And did you hear about poor old Farmer Brouwer? He met the Headless Horseman on the road. The Horseman pulled Brouwer up onto his terrible black horse and he rode away with him. He rode until he got to the small bridge near the old church. Then the Horseman threw Farmer Brouwer into the river and he rode away, making a noise like thunder."

Suddenly Brom Bones spoke.

"I've met the Horseman too," he said. "But I wasn't afraid of him. I'm a better horse rider than he is."

"Did you *really* meet him?" someone asked excitedly. "*How* did you meet him? Tell us what happened."

"I met him on the road one night," replied Brom Bones. "I asked him to race with me. So we raced our horses to the old church. But my horse, Daredevil, was faster than his horse. I won the race easily. And when we got to the bridge near the church, the Horseman disappeared in a flash of fire."

"You were very brave," said someone.

Ichabod listened to Brom Bones's story. Then he himself told a story, about evil spirits in the forest. But it was not as interesting as Brom's story. And nobody said, "You were very brave" to Ichabod.

At last, the party finished, and it was time to go home. Ichabod went to find Katrina. He wanted to spend a few minutes alone with her.

"You're looking very beautiful tonight," he told the young woman. "May I come to see you tomorrow afternoon? I want to speak to you about something very important. I want to ask you a question."

But Katrina did not look very happy or friendly. She

did not want to be alone with Ichabod.

"No, I'm sorry," she said. "I won't be at home tomorrow afternoon."

Ichabod was surprised. "Oh!" he said. "May I come tomorrow evening then?"

"No, I won't be here in the evening either," Katrina replied.

"Well, can I come the next day?"

"No, I'll be busy all this week," said Katrina. "Now please excuse me. I have to say goodbye to our other guests."

A few minutes later, Ichabod saw Katrina with Brom Bones. They were talking together and laughing quietly. Then Brom Bones held Katrina's hand and kissed it.

Katrina was looking very pleased and happy.

"What *is* happening?" Ichabod asked himself. "Does Katrina really like Brom Bones more than me? That's not possible! I can't believe it! Perhaps she wants to make me jealous."

Ichabod did not say goodbye to Katrina. He left the party quickly. He felt very sad, and he felt very angry too. He went to the stable—the place where the horses were kept—and he found Gunpowder. Gunpowder was asleep. But Ichabod kicked the horse and it quickly woke up.

Ichabod climbed onto Gunpowder's back and he rode slowly away.

6

A Terrible Race

It was almost midnight. The moon was shining brightly. Ichabod rode Gunpowder slowly along by the side of some high hills. Below him, on the other side of the road, he could see Tarry Town, on the bank of the wide, dark Hudson River. He could hear the sound of a dog barking on the other side of the river. But the sound was very far away, like a sound in a dream.

As he rode along, the schoolmaster remembered the ghost stories that people had told at the Van Tassels' party.

Suddenly, a cloud covered the moon. Ichabod felt lonely and afraid. In front of him, a huge tree stood by the side of the road. There was a very sad story about this tree. During the war between Britain and the American colony, a British soldier had hidden in this tree. His name was Major André. The man was a spy, and he was hiding from some American soldiers. Later he was captured and killed. Now, the people of the area called the tree, "Major

André's tree".

"The tree is haunted by Major André's ghost," a lot of people said.

Ichabod remembered this story, and his heart began to beat fast. He was afraid. He did not want to pass Major André's tree. But there was no other way for him to get home. So he began to sing loudly:

God will lead me safely
around this terrible tree.
No ghost or spirit
is going to frighten me—

Suddenly he stopped singing. He had heard a noise.

"What was that?" he asked himself. He looked up at the tree. Was something white hanging in it? Something white and terrible? Then he looked again. No, there was only a white mark on one of the branches.

"I'm dreaming," he told himself. "That noise was only the sound of the wind."

Ichabod passed the tree safely. But now there was another danger. This danger was more terrible than the tree. There was a forest on one side of the road. And beyond the forest, there was a bridge over a little river. The American soldiers had captured Major André on this bridge.

"Sometimes, Major André's ghost haunts that bridge at night," people said.

Ichabod wanted to ride quickly across the bridge. His heart was beating faster and faster. He kicked Gunpowder with both his feet.

"Come on, you stupid old horse," he said. "Move faster!"

But Gunpowder had a bad temper. He was not feeling happy. He did not *want* to cross the bridge. He stopped walking forwards. Instead, he turned off the road, into the forest. He ran into the forest for a few moments. Then he stopped very suddenly. Ichabod was not a good rider and he nearly fell off Gunpowder's back.

"Move, you stupid animal!" the schoolmaster shouted.

He shouted at the horse and he kicked it again and again. But Gunpowder did not move. The horse was looking at something in the forest. Ichabod looked too. His mouth became dry with fear.

A huge black shape was standing in front of him. What was it? Was it a ghost?

The hair on Ichabod's head stood up. His body shook. He wanted to escape, but the horse would not move.

"Who are you?" he whispered.

The thing did not answer.

"Who are you?" Ichabod asked again.

Still there was no answer. Ichabod began to sing loudly:

No evil thing can hurt me—

Suddenly, the thing moved. It moved out of the forest, and now it was in the middle of the road. Ichabod could see it more clearly. It had the shape of a large man on a huge black horse.

Then at last, Gunpowder decided to move. He ran back to the road. The horse ran towards the bridge. The strange Horseman waited. He did not move or speak. But when Gunpowder and Ichabod had passed him, he started to move too. He began to follow them. In a moment, he was beside them! They crossed the bridge together.

*In a moment, the Horseman was beside them! They crossed
the bridge together.*

As Ichabod rode along, the Horseman rode beside him. When Ichabod rode quickly, the Horseman rode quickly. When Ichabod rode slowly, the Horseman rode slowly. He never left Ichabod's side. It was like a terrible race.

Ichabod and the Horseman rode up a hill. Suddenly, the Horseman was in front. But at the top of the hill, he stopped his horse and waited. Now Ichabod could see the Horseman's shape very clearly against the dark-blue sky. The Horseman had no head. He was carrying his head in his hands.

Now Ichabod was really terrified—he was very, very frightened. He rode away as fast as he could. But again the Headless Horseman followed him.

At last they reached a place where a small road turned down into Sleepy Hollow. Ichabod tried to make Gunpowder turn down into the valley. He kicked the horse, again and again. But Gunpowder did not turn. He ran on past the road that went down to Sleepy Hollow.

"You stupid horse!" shouted Ichabod. "We're going the wrong way!"

Ichabod could hear the sound of the Headless Horseman behind him. The Horseman was very close.

Suddenly, Gunpowder started to run faster. That was good! But it was very difficult for Ichabod to stay on the horse's back. And at that moment, the saddle broke and it fell away from the horse. Now Ichabod had to ride without a saddle. But somehow, he held on to the horse's neck.

"That was Hans Van Ripper's best saddle," Ichabod thought. "He'll be very angry with me. But I can't worry about that now. I must escape from this terrible Headless

Horseman."

The terrible race went on. Suddenly, through an opening between the trees, Ichabod saw the walls of a building. The building was near the road. Its walls were white in the moonlight. It was an old church.

"That's the church where the Horseman's body is buried," thought Ichabod.

Just in front of the church, the road crossed a bridge over a river. Ichabod remembered the stories that he had heard at the Van Tassels' party.

"The Horseman left Brom Bones at the bridge," the schoolmaster thought. "He left Farmer Brouwer there too. So if I can reach the bridge, I'll be safe. The Horseman can't pass the bridge near the church. He'll leave me and he'll go back to the graveyard."

Ichabod kicked Gunpowder again. Gunpowder ran forward across the bridge, and after a moment they had reached the other side. Was the Horseman still behind him? Ichabod turned around.

He saw the Headless Horseman standing up on his horse. He had lifted his arm in the air. He was going to throw something at Ichabod. He was going to throw his head!

Ichabod screamed as something hit him. It made a terrible soft sound. The schoolmaster fell off the horse and lay on the ground. As he lay there, the Headless Horseman passed by him, riding as fast as the wind.

29

7
What Happened to Ichabod?

The next morning, Gunpowder was found without his saddle. The horse was quietly eating grass in a field near Hans Van Ripper's farm. But there was no news of Ichabod Crane.

Ichabod's pupils waited at the schoolhouse all morning. But the schoolmaster did not come. The boys and girls were happy to miss their lessons. They ate apples and they played on the grass near the river.

By the afternoon, Hans Van Ripper began to worry about Ichabod.

"What's happened to him?" he asked himself. "And where's my best saddle?"

Hans Van Ripper went to find some men from the village.

"The schoolmaster has disappeared," he told them. "We must try to find him."

The men looked for Ichabod for a long time, but they could not find him. At last, they went to the old church by the bridge. They found some marks in the road. They were the marks made by two horses. The marks continued across the bridge, then they disappeared in the grass.

"Look!" said one of the men suddenly. "There's the schoolmaster's hat."

Ichabod's hat was on the road near the bridge. Beside the hat, there was a very large, soft pumpkin. The big, round, yellow fruit was about the size of a man's head. It was broken.

Near the hat, there was a very large, soft pumpkin.

The water in the river was very black and deep near the bridge. Hans Van Ripper looked at it sadly.

"Ichabod couldn't swim," he said. "Perhaps he fell off my horse and drowned in the deep water. We'll look for his body in the river. But why is that pumpkin here? It's very strange."

The men looked in the river, but they could not find Ichabod. At last, they all went home. Later in the day, Hans Van Ripper searched through Ichabod's things. The schoolmaster had owned two shirts, two pairs of shoes, one pair of pants, a very old book of psalms, and a book of stories about ghosts and spirits. Hans also found some poems about Katrina Van Tassel which Ichabod had written. None of these poems was finished.

Hans Van Ripper immediately threw the poems and the book of ghost stories into his kitchen fire.

"I'm never going to send my children to school again," he said to his wife. "They don't learn anything good there. They learn about ghosts and spirits and they learn foolish poetry."

———

Soon, everybody in Sleepy Hollow had heard the story of Ichabod Crane's strange disappearance. People could not stop talking about it. What had happened to Ichabod?

Groups of people met together at the bridge by the little church. They pointed at the place where the schoolmaster's hat had been found. They remembered the stories about the Headless Horseman.

"Do you remember old Farmer Brouwer's story?" one of them asked. "And Brom Bones's story too? They both met the Headless Horseman on this road. But he left them at the bridge. Perhaps Ichabod Crane met the Horseman too. Perhaps the Horseman captured him and carried him away."

Ichabod had no family, and he did not owe money to anybody. So the people of Sleepy Hollow forgot about him quickly. Soon, another teacher came to take Ichabod's place.

———

What really happened to Ichabod Crane? The old women of Sleepy Hollow knew the answer—they were sure of that. They often told the story of Ichabod when they sat by their fires on cold winter evenings.

"Ichabod Crane was taken away by the Headless Horseman," they said. "Nobody has seen him since that night. Nobody will ever see him again."

People became very afraid of the bridge near the church. They said, "This place is haunted by Ichabod's ghost. His ghost haunts the schoolhouse too. Some people have heard a voice singing strange songs and psalms there."

On quiet summer evenings, people *did* sometimes hear strange sounds near the schoolhouse.

"Listen! Ichabod Crane is singing again," they said. "Or is it only Brom Bones's old dog?"

But there was another story about Ichabod Crane. Many years after Ichabod's disappearance, a farmer from Sleepy Hollow went to New York City. When he came back, he brought some very strange news.

"Ichabod Crane is alive," the farmer said. "I saw him in New York. I talked to him. He's a lawyer there. He's earning a lot of money."

"What do you mean?" asked another man. "Ichabod Crane is dead. He was taken away by the Headless

Horseman."

"No," said the farmer. "He left Sleepy Hollow secretly—he told me that himself. He was afraid of the Headless Horseman. And he was afraid of Hans Van Ripper, because he'd lost Hans's best saddle. He was also very angry, because Katrina Van Tassel had been unkind to him. So he did not want to stay here any more.

"Ichabod went to New York and taught in a school there," the farmer went on. "But he wanted to become a lawyer. So he studied law in the evenings."

"Is this man's story true?" the people of the valley asked each other. "Is Ichabod Crane really still alive?"

Perhaps only one person in the area knew the truth about Ichabod.

Soon after the schoolmaster disappeared, Brom Bones married Katrina Van Tassel. They were very happy together and they had many children. Whenever people talked about Ichabod Crane, Brom Bones always laughed loudly. He laughed loudest when they talked about the broken pumpkin.

Sometimes Brom's friends asked him about the night of the party.

"Do you know what really happened to the schoolmaster, Brom?" they said. "Please tell us!"

But Brom only laughed louder. *Did* he know what really happened that night? *Did* he know a secret about Ichabod and the Headless Horseman? Perhaps he did!

THE LEGEND OF RIP VAN WINKLE

1

Life in the Village

The Catskill Mountains are west of the great Hudson River, in North America. The mountains are very beautiful, but they are also very strange. The colors of the mountains are always changing. When the weather is good, they are deep blue. But often, the tops of the mountains are covered with gray clouds.

Hundreds of years ago, Native Americans lived there. These people said, "The mountains are haunted—spirits live on them. The spirits can change the weather. They can send sunshine and they can send clouds."

There are many strange stories about the Catskill Mountains. This is one of those stories. It tells about a farmer named Rip Van Winkle. Rip lived in a small village at the bottom of the mountains. The village had been built by the Dutch settlers, long before Rip was born.

Rip Van Winkle lived in the village with his wife and two children—a boy who was also named Rip, and a girl named Judith. The farmer was popular with the men and women of the village—they all liked him. He was always kind and helpful to them.

"Rip is a fine man," the villagers often said to each

other. "He helps everybody."

Rip was also popular with the children of the village. He made toys for them and sometimes he told them exciting stories about ghosts and spirits. The children often followed him around the village. Animals liked Rip too. Dogs never barked at him.

But the village women felt very sorry for Rip. The reason for this was his wife. She was quite different from Rip.

"Rip's wife is a terrible woman," the villagers said. "Why does he stay with her? She shouts at him from morning till night. She never lets that man have any peace."

This was true—Rip's wife was always angry with him. She was angry because Rip was lazy.

Rip owned a small farm but he never did any work on it. He liked an easy life. He was not interested in money. He never made any money from his farm. He never earned any money for his family.

"There's something wrong with the ground on my farm," he often told people. "Nothing grows there. The fences are always falling down. The animals are always running away. I can't work on that farm. Nothing ever goes well there."

So Rip did not work on his farm. He went fishing or he went hunting. Sometimes he even helped his friends on *their* farms. All these things made his wife very upset.

"Our farm is the worst in the country," she shouted at Rip one day. "Why? Because of you. You're lazy! It's all *your* fault! When are you going to mend the fences? Last week our cow escaped from its field again and it ate all our vegetables."

"Well, I started to mend the fences yesterday," said Rip. "But it began to rain, so I had to stop."

"And look at our children!" his wife shouted. "They're the dirtiest, untidiest children in the village. Look at their old clothes. I don't have any money to buy new clothes for them. And you don't care about that. Oh, why did I marry a lazy man?"

Rip started to move quietly towards the door. When his wife shouted at him like this, he never answered her.

"Where are you going?" shouted Rip's wife.

"It's a nice day," replied Rip. "I'm going to take Wolf out for a walk. I won't be long."

Wolf was Rip's dog. Rip and Wolf were very good friends. Rip took Wolf everywhere with him. Rip's wife hated Wolf. She often shouted at the dog and sometimes she beat him with a stick. This made Rip very unhappy. Wolf loved Rip, his master, but he was afraid of Rip's wife.

"Yes, take that dirty animal out of here!" shouted Rip's wife. "He's as lazy as you are. And don't bring him back!"

Rip was very happy to get out of the house and away from his wife. He went at once to the village inn.

———

The village inn was a quiet place. The men of the village loved to spend time there. They sat outside the inn on warm summer days and they drank beer. They told stories and they talked about all the things that were happening in the village. The inn was a very old building. On a tall wooden pole outside it, there was a picture of King George the Third.

The owner of the inn was named Nicholas Vedder. From morning till evening, he sat outside the door of the inn, under a large tree. Most of the time, Nicholas smoked his pipe and listened to his customers talking. He did not say very much himself, but sometimes he nodded his head.

The village schoolmaster, Derrick Van Bummel, often joined the group of men at the inn. Most of the people in the village could not read. But sometimes, a traveler came to the inn and left a newspaper. Then Derrick read the newspaper to the men at the inn. The stories in the newspaper were old ones. They were about things that had happened many months before. But the villagers did not care about that. They enjoyed hearing the stories.

———

Derrick read the newspaper to the men at the inn.
They enjoyed hearing the stories.

Rip Van Winkle sat down at a table outside the inn with some other men. Nicholas Vedder was not sitting under the tree, but a minute later, he came out of the old building.

"Good morning, Rip," said Nicholas. "How are you today? Would you like some beer?"

"Yes, please, Nicholas," said Rip.

Nicholas brought him a mug of beer and sat down beside him at the table. Wolf lay on the ground next to Rip.

Rip drank his beer slowly. Soon, he started to feel happy again. He began to forget about his wife.

But suddenly a hand grabbed his shoulder. A terrible voice shouted, "So here you are, you lazy, stupid man!"

It was Rip's wife. She had come to the inn to find her husband. She shouted at him for several minutes. Then she shouted at Nicholas Vedder and the other men too.

"And you men are as bad as my lazy husband!" she shouted. "You stop him from working. He comes here and he drinks beer with you. You're *all* stupid and lazy—all of you."

She pushed Rip off his chair and she pulled him home.

Rip tried to go to the inn a few times more. But his wife always followed him and pulled him home. So finally, he stopped going there. But he became very unhappy.

"What can I do?" he thought. "I can't stay in the house all day. And I don't want to work on the farm."

After that, Rip and Wolf often took walks in the forest near the village. They sat for hours under a tree in the middle of the forest. But Rip's wife always followed him and shouted at him.

_____

One fine autumn day, Rip had an idea.

"It's a beautiful day, Wolf," he said to the dog. "Let's go up into the Catskill Mountains. Let's go hunting. I'll bring my gun. Perhaps I'll shoot some squirrels. We'll have a good time in the mountains. My wife will never follow us up there. She's often unkind to you. I know that and I'm very sorry about it. But I'll always be your friend."

Wolf looked at his master and wagged his tail happily. He wanted to get away from Rip's wife too.

Rip picked up his gun. A few minutes later, he and Wolf went quietly out of the house. Rip's wife did not see them go.

2

A Strange Meeting

Rip and Wolf walked up a path into the mountains. They walked for a long time. They did not see any squirrels, but they were happy to be together. At last they arrived at one of the highest parts of the Catskill Mountains. They left the path and they found a wide, grassy place between some trees.

It was late afternoon now, and Rip was very tired. He sat down on the grass and Wolf lay down beside him. To his left, through an opening between the trees, Rip could see the green land with its little farmhouses, far below. And he could see the great Hudson River far away. The water was shining in the afternoon sun.

To his right, Rip could look down into a deep valley in

the mountains. This valley was wild and lonely. It was dark too. The sunlight could not reach the bottom of the valley.

Rip and Wolf lay on the grass for a long time. The sun started to go down and soon the air was getting cold. Night was coming. The long blue shadows of the mountains began to cover the valleys below. Smoke started to rise from the chimneys of the little farmhouses. Rip thought of his wife, who was waiting in the village. She was going to be angry with him. His heart grew heavy—he was unhappy and afraid.

At last, Rip stood up.

"Let's go, Wolf!" he said. "It's getting late. It will be dark before we get home."

As Rip turned towards the path, he heard a voice. It was coming from somewhere below him.

"Rip Van Winkle!" the voice called. "Rip Van Winkle!"

Rip looked around in surprise. "Who is calling me?" he shouted. But he could not see anybody. There was only a large black bird flying across the sky.

"I'm dreaming," he thought. "The sound was the cry of a bird, not the voice of a person. Nobody comes up here."

But then he heard the sound again. And this time it seemed nearer. It was weak and high, like the voice of an old man.

"Rip Van Winkle! Rip Van Winkle!"

"It *is* a person," thought Rip. "But how does he know my name?"

At that moment, Wolf started to growl—he made a deep, angry noise in his throat. He walked very close to his master. The hairs on the dog's back were standing up and his body was shaking with fear.

"What's wrong, Wolf?" Rip asked the dog. "Don't be afraid!"

Rip looked down into the dark valley. He suddenly saw an old man coming slowly up a steep path from the bottom of the valley. The old man was carrying something on his back.

Wolf growled again.

"It's only a poor old man," Rip said to Wolf. "But who is he? And what is he carrying on his back? I'll go down and talk to him. Perhaps I'll be able to help him."

Rip walked down the path to meet the old man. When he got near him, he stopped in surprise. The man was very short and he had thick hair and a long gray beard. But the most unusual things about him were his clothes. The men in Rip's village did not wear clothes like these. *This* man's clothes were very old-fashioned. They were like the clothes that the Dutch settlers had worn, a hundred and fifty years before.

The old man was carrying a large wooden barrel on his shoulder. He did not speak to Rip, but he made a movement with his hand. This was a sign to Rip. The man wanted Rip to carry the barrel.

"This is very strange," thought Rip. "Who *is* this old man? And why is he carrying a barrel up the mountain? I don't know! But the barrel must be very heavy. I'll help him."

Rip stepped forward and he took the barrel from the old man. At once, the man turned off the path, onto another one. This narrow path had once been a river, but it was dry now. There was no water running in it.

Rip followed the old man, carrying the barrel on his shoulder. Wolf walked by Rip's side. The old man never spoke and he never turned around.

Suddenly Rip heard a very deep noise. It was coming from somewhere above them.

"That sounds like the noise of thunder," he said to himself. "But it's a very strange kind of thunder. And there are no clouds in the sky. It isn't going to rain—I'm sure of that."

At last, Rip, Wolf and the old man arrived at the top of the path. Lots of very tall, thin rocks stood there. And there was a narrow opening between two of the rocks.

The old man walked through this opening and Rip and Wolf followed him. A moment later, Rip stopped in surprise.

They were in a wide grassy place, with tall cliffs of rock all around it. There were trees on the tops of the cliffs. The evening sun was low in the sky. It didn't shine into the grassy place between the cliffs. Rip could only see a very small piece of sky above his head.

In the middle of the wide grassy place, a group of old men were playing a game of nine-pins. They were rolling large wooden balls at nine "pins", which were like large wooden bottles. Each player tried to knock over as many pins with one ball as he could. As the old men rolled the big wooden balls, the balls made a deep, heavy noise.

"Ah! That's the noise that I heard," thought Rip. "It *wasn't* thunder. But who are these old men? There's something very strange about them."

All the men were wearing old-fashioned clothes. There were knives hanging from their belts and they wore hats with feathers. Their faces were very strange and white. One man had a very large, wide face with tiny eyes. Another man had a very big nose. They all had beards of different shapes and colors. One thin old man seemed to be the leader of the group.

For a few minutes, Rip and the man who he had met stood and watched the game.

"I've seen men dressed like this before," thought Rip. "But where?"

And suddenly he remembered.

"Yes, I know!" he said to himself. "The village school-master has an old painting in his house. The Dutch settlers brought it from the Netherlands when they came to America in 1625. These men are wearing clothes like the people in that painting. But that picture was painted a hundred and fifty years ago."

There was another strange thing about the old men. Again and again, they rolled the balls in their game of nine-pins. But they never spoke to each other. The only noise that Rip could hear was the sound of the heavy balls.

Suddenly, Rip was very frightened!

A moment later, the old men saw him and they stopped playing their game. They stared at him but they did not smile or speak. Their eyes were like the eyes of dead men. Rip's heart beat fast with fear. He wanted to run away, but his legs would not move.

The old man who Rip had followed took the wooden barrel from him. He put it down on the grass. He put some big wooden mugs next to it. He poured liquid from the barrel into the mugs. The liquid was a lovely golden color.

The other old men watched him pouring the liquid. Then the leader of the group made a sign to Rip.

"He wants me to give the mugs to all the old men," thought Rip. He quickly gave a mug to each man. They all drank the liquid in silence. Then they put down their mugs and began their game of nine-pins again. They did not look at Rip again. Soon, he began to feel less afraid.

Rip was very tired after his long walk. He was also very thirsty. He looked at the barrel, then he looked at the old men again. They were still busy with their game.

"They've forgotten about me," Rip said to himself. "I'll have a little drink from the barrel."

Rip poured some of the golden liquid into a mug and drank it. It tasted delicious.

*Rip poured some of the golden liquid into a mug and drank it.
It tasted delicious.*

"That was wonderful!" he thought. "I'll just have a little more."

Rip had another drink. Then another, and another. He filled the mug again and again. And still the strange old men went on playing their game.

After a while, Rip's eyes started to close. The empty mug fell from his hand. Then his gun fell to the ground, but he did not care. Rip could no longer stand up. He lay down on the grass and soon he was asleep.

3

Down from the Mountain

Rip woke up suddenly. He was lying in the grassy place where he had first heard the strange old man's voice. It was a bright, sunny morning and the birds were singing in the trees. High above him, a beautiful golden bird flew across the wide blue sky.

Rip's head was full of pain. He sat up and he rubbed his eyes with his hands. He remembered the strange old men with their old-fashioned clothes and their game of nine-pins.

"What happened to them?" Rip asked himself. "And how did I get back to this place? Have I slept here all night? And where is the old man with the barrel of wonderful golden liquid? Oh, why did I drink so much of it last night? What will I tell my wife?"

Rip looked around for his gun but he could not find it. But he did see a very old, broken gun lying on the grass beside him. The metal of the gun was covered with brown rust.

"Where's *my* gun?" thought Rip. "Did the old men steal it? Did they leave this rusty old gun for me?"

Then suddenly Rip remembered his dog.

"Where's Wolf?" he thought. "Perhaps he's hunting squirrels."

Rip called Wolf for a long time, but the dog did not come.

"The old men have taken Wolf too," Rip said to himself. "I'll go and find them. I'll ask them for my dog and my gun."

Rip got up slowly. He could not move very easily. As he walked, he felt sharp pains in his arms and legs.

"I don't feel very well," he thought. "I feel like an old person today. It wasn't very good for me to sleep on the cold ground last night. If I am ill, I'll have to stay in bed. Then my wife will be very angry."

Rip found the path where he had followed the old man with the barrel. But then he had a surprise. The day before, the path had been dry. But now a river was running down it. The bright clear water splashed over the rocks.

"That's very strange," thought Rip. "I didn't see a river here yesterday."

Rip climbed slowly up beside the river. At last he saw the tall, thin rocks in front of him.

"I remember those rocks," Rip said to himself. "We walked through a narrow opening between them. The men were playing nine-pins on the other side of the opening. Wolf can't be far away now."

But now Rip had another surprise. There were no

openings between any of the rocks in front of him. He looked and looked for a long time. But there was no path through the rocks.

Rip was very puzzled. "What's happened?" he asked himself. "Last night, we went through an opening between two of those rocks. And now there is *no* opening."

He called again and again for Wolf. But Wolf did not come. When Rip stopped calling, the only sounds were the songs of the birds.

By now, Rip was very hungry.

"What can I do?" he thought sadly. "I don't want to go home without my dog and my gun. But I can't stay here any longer. I need some food. I'll have to go down to the village and speak to my wife."

Rip walked down the mountain with the old, broken gun. His heart was very heavy. As he got near to his village, he met several people. But he did not know any of them. This surprised him very much.

"I know *everybody* who lives in my village—I'm sure of that," he thought. But he did not know *these* people— they were strangers. And there was something strange about their clothes. He'd never seen clothes like them before.

When the people saw Rip, they also seemed very surprised. They all put their hands on their chins. They did this again and again. At last Rip, put his hand on *his* chin too. He had a long beard!

"I didn't have this beard yesterday," he thought. "What has happened to me?"

At last, Rip entered the village. Soon, there were children following him. But they weren't the village children that he knew. They pointed with their hands at his long gray beard, and they laughed at him. As he walked through the village, dogs barked at him. He did not know any of the dogs.

The village seemed to have changed. It was bigger than it had been the day before. There were more houses and more people. Strangers' names were written above the doors of the houses, and strangers' faces looked out of the windows.

But the Catskill Mountains were still the same. And the Hudson River was still shining in the sun.

Rip was becoming more and more puzzled.

"I've been away from this village for one day," he said to himself. "But everything here looks different. What was in that strange drink last night? It has done something terrible to my mind. I've gone crazy."

Rip walked slowly to his own house. He was listening for the loud, angry voice of his wife. But his house had changed too. Nobody was living there. The roof had fallen and the doors and the windows were broken. A thin old dog was looking for food in the road outside the house.

"Can that old dog be Wolf?" thought Rip.

He called Wolf's name, but the dog did not come to him. It growled for a moment, then it walked away.

"My own dog has forgotten me," thought Rip sadly.

He went inside the house. All the rooms were empty. Rip called loudly for his wife and children. Nobody answered him. Suddenly, he felt very lonely.

"I'll go to the inn," he thought. "I'll ask Nicholas Vedder what has happened here."

Rip went to the inn. But everything there was different

too! The old building had disappeared. In its place was a large new building. Some words were written above the door. They said:

The United States Inn
Owner—Jonathan Doolittle

The great tree where Nicholas Vedder had sat every day was gone. There was a flag hanging from the top of the tall pole. Rip stared at the flag. He was astonished. It wasn't the flag of Britain. It was red, white and blue. But there was a strange pattern of stars and stripes on the flag.

"Whose flag is this?" Rip asked himself. "I've never seen it before. But the picture of King George is still on the pole too. That's *something* which hasn't changed."

But Rip was wrong. Even the man in the picture had changed. The color of his coat had changed from red to blue. He was no longer wearing a crown on his head. He was wearing a strange hat. Around the edge of the picture, there was a name in large letters—GENERAL WASHINGTON.

4
"I Don't Know Who I Am"

A crowd of people was standing near the door of the inn. Rip looked at all the people carefully, but he did not know any of them.

Rip thought about Nicholas Vedder, who often sat for hours under the tree, smoking his pipe. He thought about Derrick Van Bummel, the schoolmaster, who read everyone stories from old newspapers. Where were they?

Today, the inn was not a peaceful place. The people outside it were walking about busily. A tall man was giving notices printed on pieces of paper to the others. Everybody was talking about strange things—elections, votes, the Congress. Rip did not understand any of these words. To him, they were like words in a foreign language.

The people in the crowd began to look at Rip Van Winkle. They stared at this strange-looking man with his long beard and his rusty old gun. After a minute, the tall man walked over to him.

"Who are you going to vote for in the election, sir?" he asked.

Rip stared at the man. He was astonished. He did not understand the question, so he could not give an answer.

Then a fat man came forward. He was wearing a strange hat. General Washington was wearing the same kind of hat in the picture outside the inn. The fat man looked at Rip in an unfriendly way.

"Why have you come to our election with a gun?" he asked angrily. "Are you going to make trouble in our village?"

"No!" said Rip. "I don't want to make any trouble. I live in this village too. I'm a quiet man and I'm loyal to King George."

At once the people began to shout.

"He's a spy!" they shouted. "He's working for the British government. Take him away."

Rip was very frightened. He could not understand what was happening.

"Please listen to me," he said. "I'm not a spy. I'm looking for my friends. They always drink here at this inn."

"Well, who are they?" asked the fat man with the hat. "What are their names?"

Rip thought for a moment, then spoke again.

"Where's Nicholas Vedder today?" he said.

The crowd was silent for a moment. Then a man

replied. He sounded very puzzled.

"Nicholas Vedder? He died eighteen years ago. He's buried in the graveyard beside the church."

"Well, where's Derrick Van Bummel, the schoolmaster?" asked Rip.

"Haven't you heard about him?" said the man with the hat. "He's very famous. He joined the army at the beginning of the war. He became a great commander. And now he's in the Congress—he's a member of the government of the United States."

Rip could not understand these answers. What was the man talking about? What war? What was the Congress? And what was the United States? Also, the man had said, "Nicholas Vedder died eighteen years ago." But Rip had seen him yesterday.

Rip asked about some other friends, but none of the answers made him feel better. "They've all died or moved away," the man with the hat said. Rip was very sad. This was his village. He had lived here all his life. But now he felt like a stranger. Rip was sad, but he was becoming angry too.

"Does anybody here know Rip Van Winkle?" he shouted at last.

"Oh, yes, we know *him*," someone replied. "*That's* Rip Van Winkle, the lazy man over there by that tree."

Rip looked at the tree. A young man was leaning against it. His clothes were dirty and his hair was very untidy. Rip's mouth fell open with astonishment.

"That man is me," he thought. "I looked just like that yesterday, when I went up the mountain. But if that man is me, am I somebody else?"

"Who *are* you, sir?" the man with the hat asked Rip.

"What's your name?"

"I don't know," replied Rip slowly. "I don't know who I am. I'm not myself—I'm somebody else. I *was* myself yesterday, but last night I fell asleep on a mountain. Now someone has changed my good, clean gun into this old, rusty one. My own gun has gone, and my dog has gone too. Everything here has changed and *I've* changed. I don't know my name. I don't know who I am."

The people in the crowd looked at each other and smiled. Some of them touched their heads with their fingers.

"The poor old man is crazy," they whispered to each other.

"We must take his gun away from him," said one man. "Perhaps he'll try to shoot himself. Or perhaps he'll shoot one of us."

The people started moving towards Rip. But at that moment, a pretty young woman walked through the crowd. She was carrying a little boy in her arms. When the child saw Rip, he began to cry.

"Don't cry, little Rip!" the young woman said to the child. "The old man won't hurt you."

Rip looked at the woman. Had he seen her before? There was something about her that he remembered. And her little boy was named Rip.

"What's your name?" he asked her.

"I'm Judith Gardenier," replied the young woman.

"And what was your father's name?"

"Oh, my poor father! His name was Rip Van Winkle. One day, twenty years ago, he left our house. I was a little girl at that time. My father went away with his dog and gun and he never came back. The dog came home without him. Nobody knows what happened to my father. Some people said, 'He shot himself.' Other people said, 'Robbers killed him.' But nobody knows the truth."

Rip stared at the young woman. Now he knew who she was. She was his daughter, Judith. Yesterday, she had been a child. But now she was a fine young woman with a child of her own. The little boy was his grandson.

Rip had one more question for the young woman. He asked it very quietly.

"Where's your mother, Judith?"

"She died, not long ago," the young woman replied. "A traveler came to the village. He was trying to sell some things to Mother. But she got angry with him and she started shouting at him. Suddenly she fell dead onto the ground."

"So my wife is dead," thought Rip. "I'll never have to listen to her shouting again."

He put his arms around Judith and her child.

"I'm your father, Judith," he said. "Doesn't anybody here remember me?"

Everybody in the crowd was astonished. But a very old woman came forward and stared at Rip's face for a minute.

"Yes, it's true!" she said at last. "He *is* Rip Van Winkle. I remember his face. Welcome home, friend! But where have you been for twenty years?"

5

The Spirits of the Catskills

Rip told the people his story. He told them about the old man with the barrel. He told them about the other strange old men who had played a game of nine-pins on the mountain.

When Rip had finished, nobody said anything for a moment. But some of the people looked at him sadly and began to shake their heads.

"This old man's story is very strange," they said. "But can we believe it?"

Suddenly, one man said, "Here comes old Peter Vanderdonk. Let's ask *him* about this."

Peter Vanderdonk was the oldest person in the village. He knew a lot about the village and about the people who had lived there.

Peter was walking slowly towards the inn. When he saw Rip, he remembered him at once. Rip told his story again.

"Is this man telling the truth?" someone asked Peter.

"Yes," replied Peter. "Rip *is* telling the truth. The Catskill Mountains are haunted by ghosts and other spirits. Many strange things have happened in the mountains.

"There's a story about Hendrick Hudson," Peter went on. "He was the first European who came to this part of the country. He gave his name to the great Hudson River. Hendrick Hudson died in 1611, nearly two hundred years ago. But he still visits the Catskill Mountains every twenty years—that's what my father told me. He comes every twenty years with a group of his friends. Hendrick comes to watch over his river—the Hudson River.

"My father once saw Hendrick Hudson and his friends, high up on the mountains," said Peter. "They were wearing old Dutch clothes and they were playing a game of nine-pins. Rip's story is the same as my father's story. And one summer afternoon, long ago, I heard the noise of their game from the mountains. The sound of the balls was like thunder. I believe Rip's story. He saw Hendrick Hudson and his friends—I'm sure of that."

Rip was very happy. Peter Vanderdonk believed his story, and everybody else believed Peter. After that, the people at the inn forgot about Rip and they started talking about their election again. Judith Gardenier took her father home with her. She lived in a warm and comfortable little house. Her husband, John, was a farmer. He was a very kind and friendly man and Rip remembered him well. John and Judith had been friends when they were children.

And Rip was soon talking to his own son. He was the person who had been leaning against the tree outside the inn. He was very like his father. He did not enjoy hard work. He wanted an easy life. He had a job on John Gardenier's farm, but he never did much work there.

––––

Only a few of Rip's old friends were still alive when he returned to the village. But as time passed, he made new friends. They were the young people of the village. He enjoyed talking to them very much.

Rip lived happily with Judith Gardenier and her family for many years. He was an old man now, so nobody wanted him to do any work. He often went to the United States Inn. He sat for hours outside the door there, talking to Mr Doolittle. Rip had been away from the village for twenty years and lots of things had changed. It took Rip a long time to learn about all the changes. Many of them surprised him. He learned about the war with Britain, and about the new government of his new country—the United States of America.

Rip had a lot to learn, but he was very happy. He was free from his troubles, he could do whatever he liked. And he did not have to worry about his wife any more.

Rip told his story to every stranger who came to the inn. Soon, all the people in the village—men, women and children—knew the story well.

——

Sometimes on summer afternoons, people still hear the sound of thunder from the Catskill Mountains. "Listen!" they say to each other. "Hendrick Hudson and his friends are playing nine-pins again."

And when wives shout at their husbands, the husbands often think, "I'd like a mug of Rip Van Winkle's wonderful liquid tonight."

Points for Understanding

THE LEGEND OF SLEEPY HOLLOW

1

The Headless Horseman always rides fast—as fast as the wind.
The people of Sleepy Hollow know the reason for this. What is
this reason?

2

Ichabod Crane is a schoolmaster, but he often helps farmers
with the work on their farms. Why?

3

Why does Ichabod want to marry Katrina Van Tassel?

4

Why does Brom Bones teach his dog to make a terrible noise?

5

"I want to ask you a question," Ichabod says to Katrina. What
does he want to ask her?

6

When Ichabod gets near the bridge by the old church, he
remembers the stories that he has heard at Van Tassel's party.
Why?

7

"Why is that pumpkin here? It's very strange," says Hans Van Ripper. Why *is* the broken pumpkin near the bank of the river?

THE LEGEND OF RIP VAN WINKLE

1

Why does Rip take Wolf into the Catskill Mountains?

2

"It's a very strange kind of thunder," Rip says to himself. Why does he think this?

3

Rip wants to find the strange old men who were playing nine-pins. He wants to ask them for his dog and his gun. But he does not succeed. Why not?

4

How many people in the story are named Rip? What are the full names of these people?

5

Who has Rip met in the Catskill Mountains? Why were they there?

Published by Macmillan Heinemann ELT
Between Towns Road, Oxford OX4 3PP
A division of Macmillan Publishers Limited
Companies and representatives throughout the world

ISBN 0 333 93116 5

This retold version for Heinemann ELT Guided Readers
First published 2000
Text © Anne Collins 2000, 2003
Illustrations © Francisco Meléndez 2000, 2003
Design © Macmillan Publishers Limited 2000, 2003
Heinemann is a registered trademark of Reed Educational & Professional Publishing Limited
This version first published 2003

Illustrated by Francisco Meléndez
Cover illustration by Francisco Meléndez

Printed in Thailand

2009 2008 2007 2006 2005 2004
14 13 12 11 9 8 7 6 5 4